MW00940951

What Is A Real Man?

by

William A. McLean

Bloomington, IN  Milton Keynes, UK

authorHOUSE®

AuthorHouse™
1663 Liberty Drive, Suite 200
Bloomington, IN 47403
www.authorhouse.com
Phone: 1-800-839-8640

AuthorHouse™ UK Ltd.
500 Avebury Boulevard
Central Milton Keynes, MK9 2BE
www.authorhouse.co.uk
Phone: 08001974150

First published by AuthorHouse 10/12/2006

ISBN: 1-4259-6917-8 (sc)

Library of Congress Control Number: 2006908825

*Printed in the United States of America
Bloomington, Indiana*

This book is printed on acid-free paper.

Foreward

Will McLean and his family joined our congregation about seven years ago. Being a military family, they were accustomed to change and we know that God brought them to us with a special purpose. Since their arrival they have had a distinctive place in our hearts. He and his wife, Carolanne are exceptional musicians and they have been a great gift to us over the years. Despite the hardships of a military life, they have continued to serve faithfully and are always a blessing to those who surround them.

In 2004, McLean left our congregation to serve in Operation Freedom, Iraq. A year later, on his return, he felt God calling him to teach men about becoming **real men**. Having talked to many men during his deployment, and experienced their relationships and the trials they went through while they were separated from their spouses and families, he saw that many men are missing essential facts about what a real man is.

The book you hold reveals truths about what God created a real man to be and what He created him to do. It explains the truth about dominion, purpose, position, and the responsibilities that a real man holds. He also explains what happens when men don't take their destined positions.

Using Jesus as the primary example to follow, McLean will take you on a self-discovering journey to unearthing the definition of a **real man,** and how you can become the man that God wants you to be.

Get ready to learn about being a man blessed and favored by God among his family and his friends. But, above all, be prepared to let God transform you into the husband, father, and man that He has called you to be.

Terry W. Whitley
Pastor

Introduction

Growing up as the only boy and the youngest of two children had it's pro's and con's. As the youngest, I had the protection and support of my family. My Dad wasn't there most of the time because of work or something, but he still managed to show his support from time to time. Usually it was my Mom and my sister who supported me. They made me feel like I was the most important person in the world. They always made sure people wouldn't hurt me even if they got hurt. They did a lot of things for me. Talk about support!

The downside of being the youngest and the only boy was: I was taken care of too much and I was around my Mom and my sister most of the time. You might be thinking, "Can you be taken care of too much?" "What's wrong with being around my mom and sister?" There is nothing wrong with being around your mom and sister or anyone who loves you, but you can be taken care of too much. Why do I say this? The reason is because when you do too much for a boy that will soon become a man you train him to be lazy. Second, when a boy spends too much time around women, they become his example instead of his father. Why is this important? It is important because a woman cannot to be a man.

Now there are boys who turned out fine and some women might argue that they don't need a man to teach a boy how to become a man because they turned out so well. However, ***John 5:19 says "Jesus said unto them, I do nothing of my own accord (myself) but what I see my Father do I do."*** What was He saying? He was saying that the boy's primary example and direct guidance should come from his father. The way a boy learns how to be a man is by watching **a man**, especially his **father**, just as girls watch women to learn how they should be. Now I know that there are some situations that cannot be helped, but I am talking about those situations that can.

This was the situation I faced growing up into adulthood. I was not given proper guidance and mentoring to be a man. Today, boys and young adult males are still without guidance and are sent into the world unequipped to handle responsibility.

Consequently, this problem doesn't just affect boys, but also girls who will become women. They also grow up without the necessary information and guidance from their fathers, especially how to relate to men. I had to figure out what a man was. Most importantly, I had to find out who I was.

When I became a man and I knew who I was, God commissioned me to write this book. This book is for such a time as this. First, it is designed to help girls, who will one day become women, relate to men. Second, it is designed to help mothers relate to their sons. Third, it is designed to help women who are married relate to their husbands. Finally, it is designed to help a young boy become a REAL MAN.

Table of Contents

PART ONE

Real Man:
Myths And Truths

Here are some myths.

I am a real man because:

1. I don't cry.
2. I have a job and I pay the bills.
3. I have a car and a nice sound system.
4. I am 21 years old or older.
5. I don't get scared.
6. I tell women what to do, they don't tell me what to do.
7. I don't show emotions.
8. I know how to fight.
9. I don't need emotional support
10. I am good at sports.
11. I have sex with many girls.
12. I am good with outdoor activities.
13. I hold a major position at my job.

Have you have every heard these things? Have you ever thought these things? Better yet, have you done any of these things? If you have, then you are like a lot of people. What has happened more than we like to admit is we repeat things that we have heard and seen. Sure it seems right, but is it? Just because someone we trust has thought, said or demonstrated these myths doesn't make them true. They were sincere in their actions, but sincerely wrong. This is so common in our society and yet when someone stands up to question the validity of the information, usually they are expelled, isolated or extremely criticized for it. Most just give in and go with the flow because that kind treatment is too much to bear. They never realize that they are becoming a product of partial truths and ultimately being set up for failure.

The only way to prevent failure is to give people the truth because the truth never fails. What I mean by this is that you can rely on it. Truth does not change. It is what it is. It stays the same. Some reading this might be saying, "Everyone has his or her own truth or what he or she believes to be true, so how can you say that we must give people the truth?" Well take for example, if you were in school and the teacher asked, "Who was the first president of the United States?" Your response would probably be "George Washington." Where did you get that information? You might say, " I got the information from a history book." You just read this book and you believe that? That could be someone else's truth. You weren't alive back in those days, so how do you know what was put in the book is true? You see my point?

Now back to the myths. If I cry am I less than a man? No. I am human. So what if I can pay the bills; a woman can pay bills too! But does this make her a man? What about having a car with a nice sound system? This just means I have a nice car with some noise. If I sex with many women what do I get out of it? The only thing I get is bragging rights with the fellas, maybe a player's degree and maybe a disease. Are you getting this?

Here are some truths.

1. Most men do not know what a real man is.
2. Most women don't know what a real man is.
3. Men need emotional support.
4. Some men do not know about women or even themselves.
5. Not all men like sports.
6. Sex isn't the number one thing a man needs.
7. It takes more than being 21 years old to be a man.

Some of you that have read these statements might be saying, "You have got to be kidding?" No I am not kidding. Some readers might be shaking their heads approving of these statements. Others might be saying, "That's your opinion! Where are you getting your information?" Nine out of the ten men I talked to about being a real man agreed they didn't know about being a man. Of the woman I talked to, ten out of ten did not know what a real man was. Both the men and women I talked to all came from broken homes where their fathers were not active in their lives. Are you still saying that this is just an opinion? Can you imagine if I were to interview the whole world?

Here's more. Most men who were taught they shouldn't cry have been robbed of emotional development. They never learn how to talk about or deal with their feelings. Instead, they hold their feelings in and explode in the heat of the moment. Most of them are angry, bitter and frustrated, but don't know why. (This can also apply to women.)

When it comes to sports, it's hard to imagine that some men are not into sports. Is there something wrong with that? No. Men like what they like. There are women who like sports just as much as some men do. If you like sports you like sports. If you don't then you don't.

Now this truth is probably the most intriguing of statements. Sex isn't the number one thing a man needs. Do you need me to repeat it? Men do want sex, however, that's not the number one thing. What is the number one thing? Well, you have to read the later chapters to find out.

When I turned 21, I thought that all the information I would need automatically came with age. This is what I assumed and how wrong I was. We must be taught! We don't just grow up and the information is there. If that's the case, then why do we have schools and why do we go to them? We go to them to learn because we are born not knowing anything. As I stated earlier, we must be sure we are receiving proper information as well as giving it.

Train up a child in the way that he should go: and when he is old, he will not depart from it. (Proverbs 22:6)

Some of you guys reading this might be shaking you head affirming these statements. If you are, then I applaud you. If you find yourself getting offended, then maybe there is something you have not admitted to yourself.

As for the ladies that may be reading this, if your son, brother, or husband is experiencing these signs, then ask God for wisdom for how to help them. While they work to try to become real men, do not beat them across the head when they mess up. Encourage them. I know some of you have been waiting a long time, but if he is making progress, acknowledge it. Now I am not saying don't say anything to him because some situations require that. However, you do need to pick and choose your times wisely. It takes time to become a Real Man, even if they are over 21 years of age. Pray that God would give him wisdom and grant you understanding.

If any of lack wisdom, let him ask of God. (James 1:5)

PART TWO

What Is A Real Man?

"If you were a Real Man, you would do this and that!" These words seem to be echoed throughout our society by both men and women in every ethnic background. This statement is used too loosely and sometimes as a way of controlling men. True. There are things that make a man a man, but have you thought to ask what those things are or are you just like most folks that follow the flow without challenging the accuracy of the information? Some of the guys that are reading this might be saying, "Are you trying to tell me I am not a real man or I don't know what a real man is?" No. But, if the shoe fits… This is not to insult men, but a wake up call to examine ourselves and take our place. "What is a Real Man?" Let's define it.

Definition of a Real Man

A real man is an adult male whose body, mind, and heart has matured and embraced his position, purpose and responsibilities.

You will not find this definition in any encyclopedia, thesaurus, or dictionary. Being a Real Man is not about getting to a certain age and saying I'm here and that's it. It's more than a statement or even a definition; it is a divine appointment that requires males to be all that they were created to be.

Let's take a closer look at the definition.

Body: Meaning that he have grown to a point where all puberty phases have been completed. What does this mean? It means that his body has reached the fullness of time. He can handle his own weight. Now when God created man he made him complete and ready to handle the task of running the planet. (Read Genesis Chapter 2&3) By this I mean the physical demand that is placed on his body in taking care of the planet. We are born as babies then we grow into the framework of adulthood. When we have completely grown into this frame then we are called adults.

Mind: Meaning that he has attained knowledge and is able to care for himself as well as others. This means he has been trained about the things of life. He has some experience in being responsible. He understands he has to push beyond how he feels in order to accomplish a task. He is mature and can handle pressure until he gets the job done. Finally, he's capable of handling taking care of other people, including a family.

Heart: Meaning he has enough courage to handle knowing who he is while also allowing others to be who they are.

Courage is not about 'never' being afraid, but doing and behaving the right way even when you are afraid. Courage is required when finding out who you are because when you interact with others that are not like you, especially those with strong personalities, you may feel you have to be someone else (put up a front). You may even put some type of restriction on that person's personality without even realizing it.

Position: Lord, High priest, head of the house, leader, ruler and covering.

Seems like a lot hats to wear, huh? Well that's because it is. You see God created us in his image (Genesis 1:26) and made us just like Him. Position is everything. When we do not take our position, then there is no order. When things are out of order they do not work. You ever went to a coke machine and it says "Out of order?" It means the machine is not working, which is what is happening in the world today. Many of us are out of order.

The man is also the authority. This means dominion. We are to rule with wisdom and love. Not like a dictator or someone who feels they are the only one who knows and controls everything and everyone.

As for the covering, we are to cover our families the same way Christ covers us. We are to cover them with our love, prayers and guidance, but most of all, our obedience to God. When we do not cover them, we allow them to be attacked by the enemy. We have this position and it's not negotiable like it or not. (Read 1 Peter 3:6, 1 Corinthians 11:3, Ephesians 5:23)

Purpose: As the leader, we are to lead, and as the head we guard serve and protect.

Every man has a purpose. Everything that God has made has a purpose. For example, let's take a screwdriver. If you buy a screwdriver, you bought it because it turns screws. Wouldn't you agree? If you take that screwdriver and use it for anything other than turning screws, it would not be effective. In addition, if you take that screwdriver anywhere in the world, it will still have the same purpose. The correlation between the screwdriver and man is, if he does anything other than what he was designed to do, he will not be effective. Not to mention, if he goes anywhere in the world, even if he comes in contact with someone who can do more things than he; his purpose is still the same. When you know your purpose, you feel better about yourself and you have more confidence. You are able to lead because you have a purpose and you know where you are going.

The next thing we are supposed to do is serve our families. Men are to serve their wives not waiting to be served. Jesus said, "If anyone considers himself the greatest, he must first serve. (Matthew 23:11) Serving not only promotes humility but it brings you down to level where people are. This is how you reach them. Remember when Jesus washed the disciples feet? (John chapter 13) It also shows the person that you really care. Not only are you down at their level, but also you are cleaning a part of the body that smells and has all kind of dirt on it. There's a lot to be said for serving.

As for being the guardian, we are to keep them from things that will hurt them. If someone tried to hurt someone you were responsible for, what would you do? You would protect them right? (Read Psalms 8:3-5, Genesis 1:26, 1 Corinthians 11:3, Ephesians 5:28-29)

Responsibilities: To love and care for those that are under his dominion, be an example, maintain order, and mentor others for leadership.

The biggest of our responsibilities is to show 'love'. We do this by meeting the 'needs' of those that are under us, thus showing them how important they are. Needs include, getting a job providing for them financially and being a good steward over the resources that are given to our care. (Read 1 Timothy 5:8) We are to be their example. This means showing them what 'right' looks like. This means getting involved in their lives, making appropriate corrections, giving proper guidance and not being impatient, but loving and understanding.

This seems like a lot to be a real man doesn't it? That's because it is. We have been given a lot, so much will be required of us. (Luke 12:48) Remember, we are created in the image of God. So if God has a lot of responsibilities and we are made to be like him, then shouldn't we have responsibilities too?

Difference between boys and men

Most might say, "Why did you put this small section in here? You just defined what a real man is." Well, I think it is imperative to make a distinction between boys and men because there are men who behave like boys, and boys who think they are ready for the big time when they are not. 1 Corinthians 13:11 says, "When I was a child (boy) I acted like a child and thought like a child, but when I became a MAN I put away childish (boyish) things. Boys basically do what they want to do. They do not have their priorities in order. Now the statement I am about to make might offend some, but here it is. A boy will still let his mother, or some other woman, take care of him rather than finding a way to stand on his own two feet. BUT as soon as the women who are taking care of him, challenge him about the reason he's not able to take care of 'himself', all of a sudden the 'boy' rebels against his caregivers, demanding to be treated like a 'man'. As I stated earlier, it takes a lot to become a man. You do not fall down a 'blunder' and then become a 'wonder' nor do you switch from boy to man when it is convenient. Becoming a man is a choice made in the heart of a boy. He will eventually reach a time when his heart tells him it's time to take care of himself; time to become the caregiver.

PART THREE

God's Original Intent

In order to find out how things are supposed to be now, you need to find out how things were originally. In this I mean we must find out God's original intent for creating man.

God's intent was to create a being like him in every way. This was so important to Him that there was a discussion in heaven about it.

*"And God said Let **us** make man in **our** image".* Who was God talking to? The Bible states in 1John 5:7 *"For there are three that bear record in heaven, the Father, the Word (Jesus John 1: 1-14), and the Holy Ghost: These three are one (Unity)".* God the Father, God the Son, and God the Holy Ghost had a conference about the details of man and how to make him the best that he can be. Not only are we God's greatest creations, but also we have been destined for greatness!

How are we like God?

1. Perfect in creation: When God made us, He wanted us equipped with everything we would need to be successful. The word perfect has many different meanings and applications,

but in Hebrew it means **complete** or **whole**. Now keep in mind, 'completeness' does not mean being without flaw. When Adam was made, he was completely whole, but innocent in the same sense as a baby is innocent. He didn't know everything he needed to know, but had potential. In order for that potential to be developed, God gave him certain responsibilities.

2. Triune in make up: The word triune means " *Three*". Man was created a three-part being. *"And the Lord God formed man of the dust of the ground (body), and breathed into his nostrils the breath of life (spirit); and man became a living soul "* - Gen 2:7

"And the very God of peace sanctify you wholly; and I pray God your whole **spirit** and **soul** and **body** be preserved blameless unto the coming of our Lord Jesus Christ." - 1Thess 5:23

Body = Soma (sight, touch, taste, hearing, and smell)

Soul = Psuche (mind, will, emotions)

Spirit = pneuma (conscience, intuition, communion)

As I mentioned earlier, God exists in three persons God the Father, God the Son, and God the Holy Spirit. *"For there are three that bear record in heaven, the Father, the Word (Jesus) and the Holy Ghost: and these three are one." - 1John 5:7*

3. Dominion over all created works: Dominion here in Hebrew means *'tread'*. The word picture is: when walking on something it's underfoot. Simply put, we are in charge. *"And God said Let us make man in our image, after our likeness: and let them have **dominion** over the fish of the sea, and over the fowl of the air, and over the cattle, and over all the earth and over every creeping thing that creepeth upon the earth" - Gen 1: 26*

*"What is man that thou art mindful of him? And the son of man that thou visitest him? For thou has made him a little lower than the angels, and hast crowned him with glory and honor. Thou madest him to have **dominion** over all the works of thy hands; thou has put all things under his feet: all sheep and oxen, yea and the beasts of the field; the fowl of the air, and the fish of*

the sea, and whatsoever passeth through the paths of the seas." - Ps 8:4-8

So what does this say about God when it concerns us? It says that He wants us to be like him in every way. He has put all things under our feet. He has created us with and for a purpose. God wants us to be all that He created us to be and not an ounce less.

PART FOUR

Attacks On Men

Have you ever wondered why many men in inner cities seem to be in either one of four places; dead, on drugs, in jail or have become homosexual? Please don't get offended when I say the word homosexual. Homosexuality is not some disease that you catch or some abnormal growth in you body, but it is something that goes against God's original intent for man. You must understand God did not create men to be with men. (Read Romans 1:24, 26-28) Now when I mention the word "dead" I know some may be misunderstanding me. We all have to die and there is no changing that, but what I am talking about are the men who die before their time. I am talking along the lines of drive-by shootings, gangs and the like, which take them out before they even get a chance to live. Most of you might respond with "They are just bums who don't want to do anything with their lives." In some cases this is true, but in other cases it's not. You have to ask yourself, "How did they get this way?" The answer is they have been under attack.

Why have men been under attack?

Men have been under attack because of Satan. Who is Satan? He is the enemy of man and has been since man was created. Before God created the heavens and the earth, He created angels. Satan was one of those angels, but before this his name was Lucifer. He led a rebellion against God in heaven and was thrown out by Michael the Archangel. Why was he thrown out? Satan was thrown out because he wanted to be God. (Read Isaiah 14:11-12 and Ezekiel 28:11-19) Where did he go after he was thrown out? He came here to earth. (Read Revelation 12:7-9)

Now when God created man He gave man dominion over all the earth, including Satan. So when man sinned, he handed the earth over to Satan. Now Satan is the god of this world. (Read 2 Corinthians 4:4) So when man tries to take his proper place, which is dominion, Satan will do everything in his power to keep him from this, even if it means killing him. The reason for this is because man is a threat to his kingdom. Let's look at two stories that support these truths.

In the book of Exodus, chapter one verse eight, there was ruler in Egypt by the name of Pharaoh. Before he became the ruler of Egypt there was a man named Joseph. Joseph was second in command in Egypt and he led the children of Israel in the things of God. Joseph died and Pharaoh took over.

The first thing Pharaoh did was look at what was going on with the Israelites. He saw that they were getting stronger (growing in numbers), so he became threatened. Now the scripture says that he came to his officials and told them, "Let us deal with them wisely so if there is a war, they will not side with the enemy."

Pharaoh then sent taskmasters to deal with them harshly. He told the midwives to kill the BOYS but leave the girls alone. Why kill the boys? Why not just kill them all? Hmmm. The midwives would not kill the boys because they feared God. This made Pharaoh mad, so he killed all the boys except one, Moses, who would later grow up to deliver the children of Israel out of Egypt. (Read Exodus chapter 1-19)

The same situation happened in the book of Matthew chapter 2. There were men who were studiers of the stars and recognized the Eastern star as a symbol of the birth of a new king. They followed the star to

Jerusalem to ask Herod, the king at the time, "Where is the baby that was born to be the King of the Jews?" The first thing Herod did was get mad. Why would a King get mad over this? Herod got mad because the worship of this child threatened his position as king.

So what did Herod do? He had meeting with all of his officials to enquire where the baby was. Then he had a secret meeting with the wise men and said, "When you find out where the baby is, let me know so I may worship him." Why did he have to have secret meeting and if he wanted to worship the baby, then couldn't he have said so in the beginning? Hmmm. God warned the wise men not go back to Herod. So when Herod found out the men did not come back, he became enraged and had all the BOYS two years and younger killed. Man, doesn't that sound familiar? Of course you know the baby is Jesus, who is the Savior of the world and has delivered millions and millions of people. In fact, He's still delivering people today.

What do these two stories have in common? They both have leaders that were threatened with losing their kingdoms. They gave a decree to kill all the boys. But again why the boys? Boys one day will become men and they will rule and take dominion. When men take their dominion they have influence, and with that influence comes order. Are you getting this? If Satan cannot kill you, then he will try to do whatever he can to put you in bondage, hinder the plan of God for your life and most of all, keep you from taking dominion. Some of the tactics are so traumatic that many men never recover.

Let's look at it from another prospective. When nations had wars, the men went to fight and if the boys were old enough to fight they would go too. Most of them would not return and the remaining boys (Infant to 15) would have to assume the task of trying to be the leaders or heads of their families. This meant they would have to grow up fast. Their fathers, or some type of male figure were no longer around to give them an example to follow. Sometimes the task was too much to bear and affected their emotions. Their response to their overwhelming tasks might sometimes have been tears, like any other normal child. This is where you would begin to hear phrases like "Boys don't cry!" and "You are the man of the house!" Can you imagine being a boy with the responsibilities of a man?

Today, too early boys are having to assume the responsibilities of being men, not because their fathers or some other male figure went to war and died, but because these adult males ignored the awesome responsibility of being proper role models; being real men. When this happens, the boy grows into an adult who is unequipped to handle the task of being a man.

The Effects of Being Attacked

When these boys are attacked, they carry with them lifetime effects, and some never recover from these effects.

Now lets look at some other attacks and their effects.

Drugs: Cloud judgment and destroys the body.

Molestation: Confuses the mind and soul. Can possibly lead to homosexuality. Becomes sexually active.

Physical Abuse: Creates fear and withdrawal, becomes bitter and in many cases the abused boy becomes the abuser.

Verbal abuse: Creates resentment and fear.

Rejection: Creates low self-esteem, desperate.

Humiliation by other both girls and boys: Becomes revengeful, bitter, anger, emotional breakdown, low self-esteem.

Reading about or seeing someone have sex: Begins to have thoughts, possibly imitates what has been seen or heard. Some confusion may take place.

All of these things hinder, or stop the boy from becoming a man.

So what happens to them after all of this?

After all of this happens, the boy begins to step in adulthood and doesn't even realize that he's been under attack. Most of them just think this is 'just the way it is'. No it is not the way it is. Now I am not saying that man has an excuse for not becoming a proper man, because he doesn't. But what he does have is an opportunity, if he takes the time to learn about himself. If he does not take the time to find out about himself he will not reach his full potential. Like I stated earlier, Satan will do everything in his power to stop or hinder the boy from becoming a man and taking dominion.

PART FIVE

Man's Dominion

Throughout the book, I have been talking about dominion and it's importance. This chapter is dedicated to dominion.

The word 'Dominion' comes from the Hebrew word meaning *'tread down' or 'rule'*. The word picture here is like when a man walks on his property. He is treading on what he owns. He is the ruler! When God told Joshua (Joshua 1:3) that *"every place the sole of his foot shall tread upon, that will he give him"*, He was talking about dominion and this is the same principle in Genesis 1:26.

Where does Man's dominion come from?
Man's dominion comes from God. Genesis 1:26:

*"And God said, Let **us** make man in our image, after our likeness: and let them have **dominion** over the fish of the sea, and over the fowl of the air, and over the cattle, and over all the earth, and over every creeping thing that creepeth on the Earth."*

When God made man he wanted to make an image as close to Himself as possible. God as the creator of Heaven and Earth has dominion over everything.

He is responsible for all. This means that everything that was created by God was put under the authority of man. The only thing God required of man was to have a relationship with Him and to fulfill his responsibilities as the ruler of the earth.

Why did God give man dominion?

1. To make them (mankind) like him. Gen 1:26
2. To create a government Gen 9:1-7, Rom 13:1-6, Peter 2:13-17
3. To have authority Gen 1:26-28

Before God gave man total dominion he was put to work into the garden to serve. Gen 2:15 says, *"And God took the man and put him into the Garden of Eden to dress it and to keep it."* After he had proven himself faithful, he was given a name, Adam. Names represent titles and titles represent positions and positions represent dominion. After the title, he named the animals, showing his authority. *Gen 2:19 says, "And out of the ground the Lord God formed every beast of the field, and every fowl of the air and brought them to ADAM to see what HE would call them: and whatsoever ADAM called every living creature that was the name thereof."*

You cannot have dominion without authority. When the man was created he was made perfect. Why did God put him in the garden to work? I believe to set precedence. The precedence is: before God releases dominion to 'created beings', they must prove themselves. The parable of the talents is the precedence that correlates to this. Matt 25:14-29...

14 For the kingdom of Heaven is as a man traveling into a far country, who called his own servants, and delivered unto them his goods

15 And unto one he gave five talents, to another two, and to another one; to every man according to his ability; and straightway took his journey.

16 Then he that had received five talents went and traded with the same, and made them five talents.

17 And likewise he that received two, he also gained other two.

18 But he that had received one went and digged in the earth and hid his master's money.

19 After a longtime the lord of those servants cometh, and reckoneth with them.

20 And so he that had five talents came and brought five other talents, saying, "Lord, I have gained besides them five talents more.

21 His Lord said unto him " Well done thou **GOOD AND FAITHFUL SERVANT** thou has been **FAITHFUL** over a **FEW THINGS, I WILL MAKE YOU RULER OVER MANY:** enter into the joy of the Lord.

22 He also that had received two talents came and said, "Lord, thou deliveredst unto me two talents: behold, I have gained two other talents besides them.

23 his Lord said unto him, "Well done thou GOOD and FAITHFUL SERVANT; thou hast been FAITHFUL over a FEW THINGS, I WILL MAKE YOU A RULER OVER MANY THINGS: enter into the joy of thy lord.

24 Then the one who had received one talent came and said," Lord, I knew thee that thou

art a hard man, reaping where thou hast not sown, and gathering where thou hast not strawed:

25 And I was afraid, and went and hid thy talent in the earth: lo, therethou hast is thine.

26 his Lord answered and said "thou wicked and slothful servant, thou knewest that I reap where I sowed not, and gather where I have not strawed:

27 Thou oughtest therefore to have put my money to the exchangers, and then at my coming I should receive mine own with usury.

28 Take therefore the talent from him and give it unto him, which hath ten talents

29 For everyone who has will be given more, and he will have abundance. Whoever does not have even what he has will be taken from him.

30 And throw that worthless servant outside, into the darkness, where there will be weeping and gnashing of teeth.

This parable is talking about money, but it is also talking about dominion. How? Well, the word' talent' means money. When you look at dominion it is measured in terms of money. When you look at a corporation, the bigger it is the more money it is worth and the more 'dominion' it's owner has. When we look at the dominion of Earth, this includes all the resources; money etc. found on this planet. That's quite a figure.

Before man received total dominion, as I stated earlier, he had to work in the garden. Only the servants who worked to make their money produce were commended for their faithfulness and were rewarded. God rewarded them by giving them more dominion. Verse 21 *"Well done thou GOOD AND FAITHFUL SERVANT thou has been FAITHFUL OVER FEW AND I WILL MAKE YOU RULER OVER MANY!"*

As man was given total dominion, he was also given a name. His name is Adam, which means red, rosy, blood in the face. As I stated earlier, whenever there is dominion, there is usually a name or title. This signifies the position. Now the last servant was not faithful in his area of responsibility. Instead, he made excuses as to why he didn't do what he was suppose to. Verse 24-26

> 24 *Then the one who had received one talent came and said," Lord, I knew thee that thou art a hard man, reaping where thou hast not sown, and gathering where thou hast not strawed:*
>
> 25 *And I was afraid, and went and hid thy talent in the earth: lo, therethou hast is thine.*
>
> 26 *his Lord answered and said "thou wicked and slothful servant, thou knewest that I reap where I sowed not, and gather where I have not strawed:*

The servant was given instructions so what was the problem? He was afraid and hid. Sound familiar? Adam did the same thing. The reason both of them hid is because they were ashamed they did not obey the instruction that was given to them. "Gen 3:9-10" So what happened to the servant? He lost his talent or dominion just as Adam did.

What have you given up because you were afraid to handle your responsibilities? Four things happened to Adam when he did not take his place:

1   Afraid to oppose his wife
2   Got into idol worship
3   Lost his dominion
4   Sin enters into the world

Some men are afraid of opposing their wives because they think they will lose them. Others may not want to deal with the confrontation that could come from it. Men, if you don't correct them you will lose them anyway because no woman wants a man that they can run over. If a woman wants a man she can run over, then she doesn't want a man; she wants a boy!

Idol worship happened when Adam put more trust in his wife than in God. Adam lost his dominion, turned it over to Satan and from that point on, sin entered the world.

Having dominion is not easy. If you want it, it's going to cost you. (Luke 12:48)

Leaving the Nest

Leaving the nest is when the boy begins to enter into dominion. *Gen 2:26 says, " therefore shall a man leave his father and mother and cleave to his own wife."*

Notice only the man was told not to cleave to his father and mother.

What does this mean? It means that he leaves from under his father and goes to establish his own dominion. He has a house and job, and may eventually become a husband and then a father. As for the house, he is ruler, covering and protector, for job he is the provider, for husband he is leader, and as father he is the authority. In other words, his priorities change. He is no longer under someone else's dominion, but he is now walking in his own divine destiny.

But how does the boy get the information he needs to take his dominion? John 5:19 tells us Jesus does nothing of his own accord, but what he see his Father do, he does. This has a two-fold meaning. The first meaning states why it is important for fathers to be present. The fathers' presence is important because they are the authority in their sons' lives. Second, the way a boy becomes a man is by watching a man, specifically his father. The father is the first example and the most influential figure to his son. As human beings we are imitators of the things we see. It is so important that we are given the right example to follow. God set it up so that fathers would serve him and by serving God, they would pass information to their sons. *(Proverbs 22:6)* The only example of how to relate to God a young boy has is based on his relationship with his father. He should be able to see God in his father. Jesus made this very clear in John 14:9 *"If you have seen me, you have seen the father."* At the time he was talking to Phillip, one of his disciples, and he wanted Jesus to show him the Father. This is a direct correlation.

Does your son see God in you? If a father does not fulfill this duty, then he cannot call himself a man but an adult male. Now I don't mean that a father can't forget to tell his son some things, but I'm talking about those fathers who do not take an active role in their sons' lives.

PART SIX

Into The Heart Of Man

Now that we have defined what a real man is, discussed God's intent for creating man, revealed the attacks of Satan and man's dominion, let's now go into the heart of man and talk about his needs, challenges and his biggest fear.

His Needs

When we talk about what a man needs, some of his needs can be his wants as well.

The first need I will talk about is affirmation. A man needs to know that he is appreciated, both verbally and by action. No one wants to be used, but appreciated. This helps with his self-esteem and confidence. It lets him know how well he's doing and gives him incentive to do more. We measure our success by how well we perform. If we aren't performing well, then we have a tendency to feel that we are worthless. If you perform well one day, but not the next, does this make you worthless? The answer is no. You are still a man, but just need to make some corrections.

The next need is sex. Sex is God's plan for communication between husband and wife. Now sex is not something that men are born good at, but have to learn. I believe the best way for men to learn is by communicating with their wives. We should tell her what feels good and what doesn't. We should allow her to do the same. You see when you read books or look at some type of video, pornographically speaking, you miss out on communication and the romantic part of relating with your wife. This type of so-called 'help', does not promote a healthy sex life.

The third need is the ability to think and learn things without someone standing over him. I say this because we are designed to have dominion. Remember Genesis 1:26? There is an instinct that is placed in a man that pushes him to learn things by himself. The reason for this is because when he takes dominion, he will have to make decisions that may not be the most popular and may not get the support he normally receives, but still he must continue to do what he thinks is right. So allow your husband and sons to do things by themselves so they can prepare to handle their dominion. If you do not allow them their mistakes, then what you are doing is robbing them of their manhood. If you do this, you might as well castrate them because you make them ineffective and they will close themselves off.

Now I am not saying that you shouldn't help a man because God made you to be a helper. But if you try to help him, do not help him in everything because he may think you're a nag. You have to pick and choose your battles.

Okay, for you that have been waiting for man's greatest need, here it is. The last thing and the MOST important need a man has is the need for respect. This is the core of a man's heart. When a man does not feel like he is a man, then he will go elsewhere until he is respected. Now before anyone makes a comment, I realize that respect is not given, but is earned. A lot of men may say "You need to respect me because I am a man!" Well, if you have not taken care of your responsibilities, then you cannot call yourself a man and you will not earn respect.

Finally, when you disrespect a man, he will resent you. In some cases, you might find him to be aggressive when this happens. Basically you have told him that he is not enough man, which is the ultimate insult.

His Challenges

Being a man does come with challenges as with anything else. I believe the biggest challenge men have is with insecurity. I struggled with insecurity for 12 years and it kept me from being all that I could be. In fact, it nearly destroyed me.

Insecurity has to do with not knowing who we are. As I stated earlier, we are performance oriented. We base our self-worth on how well we perform. If we are not performing well, then we don't think much of ourselves. What we need to know is who we are. Who we are is not what we 'do' because if you lose the ability to perform, you are still who you are. For example, if Michael Jordan would've lost the ability to play basketball he would still be Michael Jordan.

People basically fall into three categories: who we think we are, who we want others to think we are, and who we really are. The first two have to do with image. This is not the same as in Genesis 1:26. "let us make man in our **image**…" Image has its place, but it can also be superficial. But who we really are has to do with character.

Man's Biggest Fear

First, let me talk about fear, (False Evidence Appearing Real) Fear is one of those things we all struggle with from time to time. God did not create man to be afraid, but he gave him power to rule the earth. (Read 2 Timothy 1:7) Fear came into the picture because of disobedience. (Read Genesis Chapter 2& 3) Since that time, man has been afraid.

So what is man's biggest fear? Man's biggest fear is that he will not be needed and that he will not be enough man for his woman. We want to be enough for our woman because pleasing her is the ultimate affirmation. This makes us feel like we know what we are doing and this gives us a huge confidence boost. It also makes us feel like a man.

The reason why fear is not a good thing is because you cannot establish a genuine relationship if you are afraid. Why? First, fear keeps you from being yourself. You act a certain way to protect your heart and emotions while only relating on a surface level. You do not get to know people by just staying at surface level, but by getting intimate. Second, fear has torment. (1 John 4:18) It condemns and plays on your mind and keeps you from asserting yourself. You become afraid of the outcome before you even start. Above all, you cannot love or be loved if you are afraid. If you cannot do either, then who will want to be in a relationship with you?

PART SEVEN

Jesus Christ:
The Model Man

.Who is your example? How did you go about picking that person? Well, when I looked for an example I could only find one that stood out above the rest, the greatest example that ever walked the earth. The man I am talking about is Jesus Christ. Jesus Christ is the perfect example because He is what we are supposed to be. How? Let's look at his life.

First, He is called the second Adam. (1 Corinthians 15:45-49) He came and restored dominion to man. He came and showed us how the first Adam should have handled business. Adam's sin caused every human being to inherit his sinful nature. In order for man to be restored to dominion, there had to be a sacrifice. But it couldn't be any sacrifice. It had to be a perfect (sinless) sacrifice and you know that there are no perfect people on this planet. In addition, the sacrifice had to be a man because it was a man that messed things up, so it had to be a man to fix things. (Luke 1:26-35)

Second, He was a real man. Although He was also God in the flesh, (Matthew 1:23) he did not get any special privileges, but suffered just like us. (Philippians 2:5-8) He knew who he was and did not allow anyone to influence him. (John 6:41, 48, 51, 8:12, 10:11,11:25,14:6) Jesus knew His position purpose and responsibilities.

His Position

Lord, Savior, Shepherd, High priest, and Head of Man, just to name a few. Do any of these positions sound familiar? He didn't just get these positions just because He was the Son of God. He was also God in the flesh. (Matthew 1:20) But this doesn't mean he had special privileges. He had to suffer just like everyone else. He had to prove himself before these titles were given to Him.

You see even Jesus learned. What? You never heard this before? Remember, Jesus was born as a baby, which meant he had to be taught, given guidance, and even corrected. Now some of you are saying "Hold up. Jesus is perfect!" Yes he is, but in the sense that He is without sin. When a person is without sin, they are perfect. We are told that He increased in wisdom. (Luke 2:52) The word increase means to get bigger or larger. So from this, we see that Jesus learned.

His Purpose

As Lord, He came to rule and reign over the earth. This means dominion. (Luke 1:26-33) Sound familiar? He brought righteousness to us through His Lordship. As Savior, He came to free us from the bondage of sin and save us from death. In addition, He came to give life. (John 1:29, 10:10) As shepherd, He came to watch, care, and nurture us. Also, He provides for our needs and protects us from the enemy. (John 10:11-16) As High priest, He acts as a mediator between God and us. He intercedes on our behalf. Most important, He gives us access to the Father. (1 Timothy 2:5, Hebrews 7:11-8:6) Lastly, as Head, He gives us direction, shows us what right looks like, and corrects us when we are wrong.

His Responsibilities

Jesus responsibilities were to teach, serve and to reach those that were lost. He taught love, forgiveness, responsibility and kingdom principles. Jesus came to serve people. Jesus said "The greatest is the one who serves the most." True servant hood implies humility. When you are humble, God not only gives you grace, but exalts you. (Mark 9:34-35, Luke 22:27, James 4:7)

Finally, He evangelized. He traveled all over world to reach those who did not know the gift of God, which is eternal life. (John 3:16, Matthew 18:11)

During his time on earth, Jesus never neglected his position, purpose, or responsibilities. He did exactly what His Father instructed Him to do. He was driven by God's instructions. In fact, He made a very powerful statement. *"My meat is to do the will of the Father."*(John 4:32-34) What does meat represent? It represents food and you know we need food to live. He was saying not even food was as important as doing what God asked him to do.

But just as we need food to live we also need positions, purposes, and responsibilities to challenge us. If you are going through life without being challenged, chances are you are dying.

PART EIGHT

Taking You Place

You have read this book and have received some of the information you need to take your place. Why must you take your place? You must take your place because there must be order. Remember, if things are out of order then nothing works. When God created the heaven and earth, he also created an order. In 1 Corinthians 11:3 the order is defined; God is the head of Christ, Christ is the head of man and man is the head of woman. When there is order, then things are able to flow.

Let me explain what happens when we men are out of order. The Bible states in Romans 5 that by disobedience (not taking his place (See Genesis chapters 2 and 3)) of one man (Adam) sin and death entered into the world, but through the obedience of one man (Jesus Christ) we receive eternal life. Want more proof?

In Joshua chapter 7, there was a man by the name of Achan who took the forbidden treasure after Israel won the battle at Jericho. Achan's disobedience (sin) caused his entire family to be stoned. Had he simply obeyed the instructions he was given, his family could have lived. This is the perfect example of why it is important for men to take dominion; take their place.

I can't stress enough how important it is for you to know and understand your position, purpose and responsibilities. You can't be a leader and not know what you are supposed to be doing, the reason(s) for doing it, and how to do it, if you are going to take dominion. You must know who you are and the only way to know who you are is to go to the one who created you, which is God.

Some might be saying, "Why do I need to go to God? I know who I am." Have you ever tried to use a butter knife in the place of a screwdriver? Does it work? You might say, "Sometimes." Okay, why does it only work sometimes? Your response might be, "The reason the butter knife only works sometimes is because it is NOT designed for that task." The reason you should seek God is because you might be trying to do the job of a screwdriver when you are actually a butter knife or vise versa.

Look at *Jeremiah 1:5 "Before, I formed thee in the belly I knew thee…"* The Bible says God knows how many hairs are on your head and they are 'numbered' not 'counted'. (Matthew 10:30) The difference is, if strands of hair fell out and you were counting it would be one, two three etc. Now if you were numbering it would be hair number 4,897, hair number 207, and hair number 8,000. You understand? So God knows you and what He has created you for.

Finally, you must be willing to commit once you have started the process of becoming a 'real man'. Don't be a butter knife trying to do the jobs of a screwdriver. Let this book be the beginning of finding out who you are. Again, be willing to commit once you start the process and don't walk away from your commitment, even if you see everyone else do it. Show the maturity and character you were designed for. Do whatever it takes (within God's design) to see this extremely important process through to the end. Stand up and take your place as a REAL MAN!

PART NINE

Invitation To Salvation

Now that I have given you information on being a real man, I want to give you an opportunity to receive Jesus Christ as your Lord and Savior. It's as easy as A, B, C. Admit that you are a sinner. Romans 3:23 says, *"All have sinned and fallen short of the glory of God."* Believe that God sent his son Jesus to save us from our sins. John 3:17 says, *"God sent his son not to condemn the world but that the world, through Him might be saved."* Confess you sins. Romans 10:9-10 says *"If you confess with your mouth the Lord Jesus Christ, and shall believe in your heart that God has raised Him from the dead, you will be saved; for with the heart man believes and with the mouth confession is made unto salvation."*

Using these scriptures say the following confession:

God I know I am a sinner. Right now I turn away from my sins and turn to you. I believe you sent your Son to save me. I believe He suffered and died to pay for my sins. I believe you raised him from the dead. I accept your son Jesus as my Lord and Savior. Please, come into my heart!

If you have said these words for the first time, I want to welcome you into the family of God. Now that you are in the family, I highly encourage you to find a church that teaches the Word of God in full authority to help you with your new life, and get yourself a good Bible.

Acknowlegdments

If I were to name everyone who influenced me, I guess I would be writing another book, but I would like to thank the following:

My Lord and Savior, Jesus Christ, without Him I would not be where I am; my father, the late William A. Evans, you were my hero and friend; my wife, my Angel, my princess, Carolanne who has supported me for all these years, I love you; my sons William and Brandon, I am proud of you always; my mother Annie L. Hinnant; my Sister Eugenia Holley, love you so much! James T. and Cora Lee McLean, my grandparents; Pastors Terry and Jan Whitley, thank you for believing in me and giving me the chance to share my heart; Steve and Pam Timmerman; Brian Leichty for your inspiration; my Grace Christian Center family; Josiah and Martina Martin; Joanne Fuller; Sylvia Petty; Tim Woodson for the words he spoke into my life and all those who took the time to listen to what I had to say. If I didn't mention you please charge it to my head, but not my heart.

About The Author

William McLean is married with two children and currently serves in the United States Armed Forces. He and his family are members of Grace Christian Center.

Terry Whitley is the Senior Pastor at Grace Christian Center.

For more information on Grace Christian Center visit www.gracechristiancenter.com

To purchase additional copies of this book, visit

www.whatisarealman.net or www.authorhouse.com

Made in the USA
Las Vegas, NV
13 December 2022

62398986R00050